By 2003, airplanes had been around for 100 years

Airplanes

Jean Allen

A⁺

Smart Apple Media

COPYRIGHT

✍ Published by Smart Apple Media

1980 Lookout Drive, North Mankato, MN 56003

Designed by Rita Marshall

Printed in the United States of America

✍ Photographs by Artemis Images (ATD Group), Corbis (Matthias Kulka), Richard Cummins, The Image Finders (Novastock), North Wind Picture Archive, Science Photo Library (NASA), Tom Stack & Associates (Charles Palek), John Wilson

✍ Library of Congress Cataloging-in-Publication Data

Allen, Jean, 1964– Airplanes / by Jean Allen.

p. cm. – (Great inventions) Includes bibliographical references.

Summary: An introduction to the ideas and technical developments that produced today's airplanes. Includes a "hands on" activity.

✍ ISBN 1-58340-321-3

1. Airplanes—History—Juvenile literature. [1. Airplanes—History.]

I. Title. II. Great inventions (Mankato, Minn.).

TL547.A613 2003   629.133'34'09–dc21   2002042780

✍ First Edition 9 8 7 6 5 4 3 2 1

Airplanes

Reaching for the Sky

For most of human history, the idea of people flying was little more than a dream. Transportation methods were simple. People walked or rode horses or other animals. If they had a great distance to cover, they rode in animal-drawn wagons or traveled in boats. In the 1800s and 1900s, inventions came along that improved transportation. Steamships, trains, and automobiles made travel much faster and easier. But through it all, people remained fascinated with the idea of

This gas-filled airship was built in Britain around 1905

flying through the air like birds. When the gas engine was invented in the late 1800s, airplanes finally became possible.

The first powered airplane flight was made in 1903 by two brothers, Orville and Wilbur Wright, who had studied how birds flew. The flight of their plane—called the *Flyer*—lasted just 12 seconds, but it changed the world. Flying was no longer a dream. It was real.

In 1162, a man in Turkey tried to fly off a tower using fabric wings. He fell to his death.

The *Flyer* was a simple plane that could not fly very far

Charles Lindbergh, the most famous pilot in history

How Flight Works

Four basic forces are involved in flight: lift, thrust, weight, and drag. Lift is an upward force. It is created by air passing over and under an airplane's wings. Thrust is forward motion. It is created by a plane's **propellers** or engines (which push, or "thrust," the plane forward). Weight is the downward pull of the airplane and its load. Drag is the force of the air trying to slow the plane down. 🖎 Many things affect these forces, such as the shape of the airplane, its speed,

The world's first hot-air balloon flight took place in France in 1783.

and even the amount of moisture in the air. The basic idea,

though, is that an object can fly if lift is greater than weight,

and if thrust is greater than drag.

Airplanes can fly because of lift—air that "lifts" the wings

Airplane Milestones

The first airplanes could not fly very far or go very high.

But as scientists learned more about how flight works,

they were able to develop faster, better **In 1927, an American named Charles Lindbergh became the first person to fly alone across the Atlantic Ocean.**

planes. During World War I (1914–18), armies around the world wanted to use planes to attack their enemies.

Thousands of planes were built and used in **dogfights** in the

skies over Europe. Airplanes continued to get better

during World War II (1939–45). A jet-powered airplane was

built in Germany in 1939. Instead of propellers, it used jet

propulsion to move forward. A pilot could fly the plane more

than 400 miles (644 km) per hour. It did not help Germany

Most planes built before World War II had propellers

win the war, but it did change the future of airplanes.

Airplanes were not used just in the military, though. Passenger

airplanes, or airliners, became common in the 1930s, when

people began to fly in large numbers. The **In 1947, pilot**

Chuck Yeager

first airliners were small and slow. But **became the**

first person to

improvements were made every decade, and **fly faster than**

the speed of

today there are many kinds of aircraft. The **sound.**

fastest airliner is the Concorde, which can fly up to 1,350 miles

(2,160 km) per hour!

Chuck Yeager, the first man to break the sound barrier

Other Types of Flight

The history of flight includes not just airplanes, but other kinds of flying machines as well. During the early part of the 1900s, giant airships filled with hydrogen (a gas) became very popular. They moved more slowly than airplanes. Then the great airship *Hindenburg* exploded in 1937, killing many passengers. That disaster ended the production of airships.

In 1939, Igor Sikorsky, a Russian living in the United States, built the world's first single-**rotor** helicopter. Within 10 years, helicopters were used around the world. Unlike most

airplanes, helicopters can **hover** over one spot and move

straight up and down. They are used for many things, from

reporting on traffic to rescuing people at sea. During the

Helicopters are slower than planes but have more uses

last 50 years, people's dreams of flight have stretched all the way into outer space. In the 1960s, the United States and the Soviet Union sent many rockets and astronauts into space. In 1969, Americans Neil Armstrong and Edwin "Buzz" Aldrin were the first people to walk on the moon. Today, space travel continues with the space shuttle. Airplanes, helicopters, shuttles, and other flying machines are among humans' most amazing accomplishments. What could be next?

In 1986, a plane called the *Voyager* flew all the way around the world without landing or refueling.

Shuttles fly into outer space with the help of big rockets

Engine Thrust

You can demonstrate how jet engines use thrust to push an airplane forward with the following experiment.

What You Need

A tube from an empty roll of toilet paper
Thin cardboard
A balloon
Double-sided tape
Scissors

What You Do

1. Cut airplane wings and a tail out of the cardboard and tape them to the tube.
2. Put a piece of tape on the underside of the tube.
3. Blow up a balloon and pinch the end shut with your fingers.
4. Stick the balloon to the tube.
5. Let go of the balloon. Watch your jet fly!

What You See

The air rushing out of the balloon is like a jet engine pushing a plane through the air. Try leaving more or less air in the balloon. What happens?

Powerful engines give today's large planes their thrust

Index

Words to Know

dogfights (DOG-fites)—fights in the air between two or more small airplanes

hover (HUH-vur)—to stay in one place in the air

jet propulsion (JET pruh-PUL-shun)—to move by pushing a stream of hot gas in the opposite direction

propellers (pruh-PEL-urz)—rotating blades that move air to create thrust, or forward motion

rotor (ROH-tur)—the turning blade that lifts a helicopter

Read More

Scarry, Richard. *Richard Scarry's a Day at the Airport*. New York: Random House, 2001.

Stickland, Paul. *Planes (On the Move)*. Milwaukee: Gareth Stevens, 2001.

Stille, Darlene. *Airplanes*. Mankato, Minn.: Compass Point Books, 2001.

Internet Sites

How Stuff Works: Airplanes
http://www.howstuffworks.com/airplane.htm

Science Fun with Airplanes
http://www.ag.ohio-state.edu/~flight/homepage.html

How Stuff Works: Helicopters
http://www.howstuffworks.com/helicopter.htm

Paper Airplanes You Can Build
http://www.paperplane.org/